The Sea Priestess's Book of Spells

By: Katie McBrien

I dedicate this book to:

Hekate, the Greek Goddess of Witchcraft,

the ocean, and the crossroads.

Without Hekate's guidance and love this book

would never have been possible.

& my best friend

it's through him I learned to move past my fears

and step into the unknown fearlessly.

The first edition published in 2018 by Katie McBrien

Copyright © 2018 by Katie McBrien

All rights reserved. No part of this publication may be reproduced or transmitted in any form or by any means, electronic or mechanical, including photocopying, recording or by information storage and retrieval system, without permission in writing by Katie McBrien. Reviewers may quote brief passages.

Cover Design by: Katie McBrien
www.katiemcbrien.com.

Table of Contents

Introduction

The Basics

    Keys to Successful Spellcasting

Home & Family Spells

    A Spell to Encourage Trust

    A Spell to Diminish Nightmares

    A Spell for Peace of Mind

    A Job Spell

    A Spell for Those Affected by a Natural Disaster

    A Chant for Peace

    A Home Protection Spell

    A Peaceful House Potion

Health Spells

    A Health Spell

    A Healing Chant

- A Spell for a Serious Illness
- Herbal Spell Bottle for Health
- A Simple Self-Healing Spell
  - Variation for those who can't take baths

Love Spells
- A Charm Bag for Love
- See Me Spell
- Aphrodite Love Spell
- A Love Chant
- A New Year's Eve Love Spell
- A Spell Bottle for Love
- Love Spell

Protection Spells
- Banishing Incense
- A Spell to Break Ties
- A Protection Chant
- A Weather Protection Spell

- A Spell to Sever Ties
- A Spell to Rid Yourself of Someone Who Needs to Go
- A Traditional Witches' Protection Bottle
- Protection and Banishing Jar
- A Banishing Spell

Sea Witchery
- A Sea Witch Harassment Chant
- A Sea Witch Protection Chant
- A Sea Witch Self Love Spell
- A Sea Witch Empowerment Chant
- Ocean Wish Spell
  - At Home Adaptation
- Sand Dollar Money Spell
- A Sea Witch Money Spell
- A Sea Witch Psychic Chant

Wealth Spells
- Enchanted Pennies

A Money Chant

Quick Cash Spell

A Money Potion

Money, Money, Money!

A Holiday Shopping Spell

Increase My Cash Spell

Money Oil

A Fortune Chant

Conclusion

About Katie

Introduction

Welcome to The Sea Priestess's Book of Spells!

This book has been in the making for years, these spells are tried and true spells that I have done myself and continue to use to this day!

This book doesn't teach magickal theory or how to cast spells, it assumes the reader has some basic understanding of magick and witchcraft. If you're new to the craft and my book is the first you've picked up; *I am honored*!

I wish to recommend the books "**The Craft of The Wild Witch**" by Poppy Palin & "**To Stir a Magic Cauldron**" by Silver Ravenwolf as books to begin your magickal path with.

I am here for my readers; feel free to send me an e-mail anytime: questions@katiemcbrien.com.

So, without further ado, contained within these pages are spells for love, money, health, and more some even with a Sea Witch flair! I hope you enjoy!

The Basics

Keys to Successful Spellcasting

Though I refer to Witches in the feminine sense, I am not excluding males. There are many wonderful male witches out there.

Here are some bullet idea's to further build upon creating successful spells to manifest your desires and wishes.

- Your "will" is the most important tool. If you know *beyond a shadow of a doubt* that your magick will succeed then you're on your way to successful spell casting.

- Tools and hard to find ingredients are just pluses as I mentioned in key one the will of the witch makes the magick. A real witch needs nothing more than a desire and strong emotions to create powerful changes in her life.

- Some spells will need to be re-enforced over a period of time. These include spells for big items such as a house, car, new job, raise, spells that influence other people, etc. Repetition is the key to success….

- All spells bend reality, but reality is much more fluid than we give it credit, think of the matrix- if you have not seen the movie do yourself a favor and rent it. However, remember that while on earth there are some things that cannot change- you will always remain physically a human (mentally & spiritually you are free to explore other "bodies and realities" look into shape-shifting and shamanic journeying), you are bound to the laws of physics- no flying……, all manner of beasts and creatures exist, just not on this physical plane, however- look into shamanic "worlds" understand that the worlds do co-exist and just like the matrix sometimes they overlap and things get a bit screwy. ((mermaids, faeries, elementals, ghosts, werewolves, vampires, etc…..))

- The most powerful witch, is not someone else with a higher degree or more knowledge, it's the witch with the emotional tie to the situation! You are the expert! Your emotions and "will" fuels each spell you cast, if you aren't into your magick, chances are it will NOT manifest. Another witch, has a chance but the best chance for success comes from your need and desires.

- A real Witch **never stops learning**, **never stops trying to improve her craft**, but she doesn't let her inexperience stop her from trying- just like learning to walk or ride a bike or write, practice makes perfect, and sometimes we have to stumble and fall before we can be a master.

> *Real Witches are spiritual athletes they may stumble and fall but the true witches get right up brush off the dirt and get right back to try again.*
>
> *- Katie McBrien*

- When your magick fails, sit back and do some journal work look at the time and phase of the moon, your frame of mind, your emotions- did you not get emotional about your need? If not, you are missing a key to success! After reflection- rework your spell on paper- look at the moon, the day, the hour, the tide (if you're a Sea Witch), and when the time is right re-work your spell(s). Most of the time the blockages exists within us or we are impatient and need to keep working the magick.

- When crafting spells, some require you to be real specific about the time frame, if you need 100$ by the end of the month be sure to state that otherwise you 100$ may come after your need has passed. You can always write down what you need and when you need it on a piece of paper and burn it or keep the paper on you.

- DO NOT BE AFRAID TO ADAPT OTHER PEOPLE'S SPELLS TO SUIT YOUR NEEDS, TIME, INGREDIENTS, BUDGET, ETC. Just because the high priestess of the coven of Avalon (or whatever) wrote the spell does not mean it's more powerful, or is going to work for you, a real witch adapts spells & rituals to their needs- always.

I hope these little thoughts will help you to master the art of spell casting.

Home & Family Spells

A Spell to Encourage Trust

A reader e-mailed me about a situation they were having about lost trust. This spell will help you regain trust with a special person(s) after you may have abused it. Remember, the most powerful force in trust magick is ***sincerity and understanding*** of what caused the trust to leave in the first place, and the sincerity that you will do your best not to abuse the relationship again.

Items Needed:

- A Piece of paper
- Pen
- A Yellow Candle
- Matches
- Candle Holder
- A bit of Heal-All herb or Rosemary (the substitute)

Timing: Waxing to Full, Full Moon.

For this spell you will be writing a heartfelt note to those who you have wronged, there is no place for ego within this note so be sure to put yourself aside be able to feel from the person's point of view who you have wronged. First gather the above required items, and light the candle with this phrase:

> *What I have done is wrong and*
> *for that I am unhappy*
>
> *What I did was not thoughtful in*
> *fact it was quite crappy*
>
> *our friendship I hope to repair*
> *with this heartfelt confession.*
>
> *I do hope eventually you will be*
> *able to look past my*
> *transgression.*
>
> *When you are ready let's move*
> *past this as one*

*knowing that what is done is
done and healing now has
begun.*

When you have said the above rhyme several times, begin to write your letter. When you are done read it out-loud with as much emphasis and emotions as possible, if you need to cry, or release the burden of guilt you hold on this situation now is the time to do it. Let your ego move out of the way. Bless the letter with the candle flame (you can pass it over top several times quickly as not to catch fire to the paper or burn it), then bless it with the heal all herb (or rosemary).

Take the used herbs outside and release them to nature. Now give the letter or mail it to the person you need to apologize too. Remember though that it is now in the other person's court and sometimes they will need longer to heal from this- if you want you can repeat this spell, but rather than sending the same note over and over again you can burn the letter and release the cooled ashes to the wind. Give your loved one a chance to heal and do everything in your power to regain their trust- it will take time.

A Spell to Diminish Nightmares

A follower asked me for a spell to help her with her nightmares, I hope this spell helps.

Items Needed:

- Amethyst crystal
- A small dish of salt water
- A pen and paper

Timing: Whenever is needed but waning moon will work best.

Location: Bedroom where you sleep.

Gather the required ingredients and prepare yourself as you normally do for magick. Begin by creating a sacred space, you can do this by sprinkling a bit of the salt water around the perimeter of your bed. I like to use this chant, but you can use whatever one you wish:

Salt water cleanses it all it meets

evil and negativity it defeats.

When you have created a sacred space, do the same procedure for the amethyst crystal, sprinkle salt water on it while intoning a cleansing chant of your choice. When that is cleansed it is time to program the crystal.

To program a crystal, hold the crystal in your dominant hand, whichever one you write with. Close your eyes and begin to see energy coursing through your body. What color does positive dreams and no nightmares look like to you? Is it pink? Is it purple? See this energy begin to take that color. When you are ready send that colored energy into the crystal.

You can also say an affirmation such as this:

_____ color brings me peace (insert the name of your color)

bad dreams and nightmares will decrease

I am free from troubled thinking

with my nightmares rapidly

shrinking.

Send the energy into the crystal, when you are ready place the crystal within your pillowcase and go to sleep. If you happen to wake up with a bad dream right it down immediately all the details you remember, in the morning take the salt water and sprinkle the paper and then tear it up and place it within the trash. Within a moon-cycle you should see positive results.

You may need to repeat this spell nightly for a period of 20-30 days if the nightmares are especially hard to get rid of remember- keep your thoughts positive and light as you fall asleep. I am a believer our dreams are a reflection of our inner world if your inner world is dark and dreary your dreams will take on that tone as well.

A Spell for Peace of Mind

Use this spell when worries and anxieties begin to get to you.

Items Needed:

- A Black Stone

- A Clear Quartz

Timing: Whenever, but best in the morning hours or before you set off on your day.

Holding the black stone in your hand begin to tell it your worries and anxieties either out loud or in your head. When you can think of no more say these or similar words:

Black sucks the bad inside

Taking it away and making it subside

What was troubling me is gone from me

As I will it so mote it be!

When you are ready place the black stone down and pick up the clear quartz, begin to think of positive things, solutions to your worries and anxieties, when you are ready you can say these or similar words:

Clear quartz empowers my soul

Making me happy, confidence, and whole

I can quickly do whatever needs to get done

Leaving me time to have some fun

Pocket the quartz crystal and go about your day. Be empowered!

A Job Spell

Use this spell to help you find a job and get it!

Items Needed:

- a white candle
- candle holder
- matches or lighter

- a piece of paper
- a green crayon, marker, pen, or pencil.
- fire safe dish or cauldron
- a mojo bag- green, red, or white.

Timing- Waxing Moon; Sunday (success + energy), Tuesday (added power & energy), or Thursday (money & finances).

Gather your required items & tools. Think about the working at hand and prepare yourself as you normally would. Holding the white candle in your hands begin to focus on the type of job you wish to attract. See this job as clearly as possible- try not to focus on a particular location- however in some cases this is unavoidable. You can say the following as you light your candle, igniting your candle and your focused intent into motion:

The perfect job comes to me

I am the best candidate I guarantee

This candle fuels my spell

insuring that all will be well

Now with your candle lit- take the paper and write out:

- what the perfect job to you is

- how far away this job should be

- what makes you qualified for this job- be sure to only list skills and credentials that you REALLY have, this is important!

- how much you wish to make (be sure to put at least in front allowing for the universe to possibly provide you MORE!)

- The hours you wish to put into work- this is important sometimes with the invention of smartphones and laptops even though your day may finish at the office at 3, you may be expected to log in and check e-mail several times throughout the night or take some work home….

- when you wish to start this job! (exact dates or time frame written out)

Now that you have the perfect job spelled out in detail. Read this list out-loud with confidence the same confidence you will use during the interview process, put that smile on your face and imagine the interviewer(s) sitting in front of you. Use your charm!

When you have completed the list say these or similar words:

> *Written on this paper is the job I*
> *wish to obtain*
>
> *with my skills and money, I wish*
> *to gain*
>
> *I am the perfect fit for this place*
>
> *you will know as soon as you*
> *see my face*
>
> *I am the perfect worker you*
> *dream about*
>
> *and with my resume there will*
> *be no doubt*
>
> *the job comes quickly to me*

as I will it so mote it be!

Remember that this spell talks about your skills, if you lie on your resume or the written paper- this spell WILL backfire on you and could cause serious repercussions!

Now BURN that paper! As you watch the fire burn you can say these or similar words:

Fire burns my spell into my field

and now the spell is sealed.

When the candle has burn out and the ashes cooled gather up the remains and place them within the mojo bag, you can add in a bit of high john the conqueror oil or root inside the bag if you have any. Carry this bag with you to your interview!

A Spell for those Affected by a Natural Disaster

Items Needed:

- A White Candle
- Matches
- A piece of paper
- A red marker

Timing: Whenever needed, though the timing is best on a Tuesday during a waxing moon in the late morning or around noon.

Background: When I think about disaster relief I think about the Red Cross, for this spell we are going to be drawing the "Red Cross" (you don't need to include the words) on a piece of paper, on the back of the paper write out the location, and "getting to safety & receiving all aid needed" then on top draw the rune Uruz:

for speed & action. You can & should use the same red marker you used to draw the red cross to draw the rune. Red is the color of action & speed.

The Spell: Prepare yourself as you normally do for spell work, by either showering and cleansing yourself or just smudging yourself with white sage or smokeless sage mist. Set out your tools and hold the candle in your hands. See the end result of your spell so in this case, we would be thinking about all those affected by the disaster getting the aid they needed and getting to safety- so this means being found, getting shelter, getting fresh food and water, and receiving any medical attention needed. When you have visualized the outcome, charge your candle with these or similar words:

Disaster has struck people are

in need

relief must come with great

speed

those who can will provide their

aid

insuring that life-giving support

shall be made

When the intention has been set light the candle while saying these or similar words:

Intention is set and fire propel

Insuring the success of this

important spell.

Taking the marker & paper, draw the cross, write the intention and draw the rune on top. fold the paper three times towards you, and then place it underneath or near the candle. Allow the candle to burn completely out. Keep the remains until you are satisfied that the relief has come to the level you desire- repeat as needed. Remember this:

Intention is the most important part of any spell, regardless of timing or the items on hand. Set the intention, will into being, and magick is made!

A Chant for Peace

Use this simple chant to help you reaffirm peaceful energies in your life. You can use this before a hard conversation, or perhaps after a fight.

Love is the answer it brings the light

it clears up the energies after a fight

any energy that may bring harm

will not be able to handle this little charm

Goddess brings love and peace here now

peace, love, and happiness are what I allow.

anger begone, sadness begone,

frustration be gone.

A Home Protection Spell

Items Needed:

- 1/4 cup of Salt
- 1/4 cup Dried Rosemary (The witch's herb)
- A glass or metal bowl
- Mortar and Pestle
- Black Candle (protection) or a white candle with the Rune:

-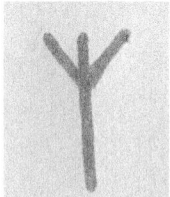

- Matches

Timing: The timing for this spell should be somewhere between New to Full Moon because we are increasing our protection.

Prepare your space, and then yourself for magick in whatever way you see fit. Taking the candle with the Rune Algiz carved on it empower it by speaking out its purpose:

A Candle to light the way

to greater protection and safety

today

Black all the colors mixed in

one

adding their energy until the

spell is done

Taking bowl add in the rosemary and the salt mixing it thoroughly with your hands. See your energy mixing with the rosemary and salt, when you feel you have done this step thoroughly adding a bit at a time to the mortar and pestle grind up the mixture into a powder. As you grind in a clockwise fashion (to empower and bring up the energy) say these or similar words:

Two worlds brought together;

earth and sea

Bringing the strongest

protection to my family(me)

A powder to go around my

belongings and home

to create a protective dome.

herbs and salt and a candle to

light the way

strong protection night and day.

After you have crushed all the mixture take the mixture and sprinkle it on the door ways, windowsills, and walk around your house three times sprinkling the mixture it doesn't need to be a lot, a little bit will do. Then walk around to the places you have deposited the salt with the candle.

Place the candle in the center of your living space and close your eyes. Visualize the salt rising and creating a protective dome around your living space and property.

For some the 1/4 cup of herb and salt may not be enough so increase or decrease as needed. If you have an apartment sprinkle this on your windows, closets, laundry room (the dryer often has a vent that leads outside) and near the central air ducts. Sprinkle a fair amount near your front door and if you must vacuum it up only after it has sat for at least three hours. You can always say it's homemade carpet deodorizer. If you have hardwood floors add a pinch to a bucket of water and mop you front doorway threshold.

A Peaceful House Potion

This potion is going to be used to help keep peaceful energies around the house; you can anoint thresholds (magickal places indeed), door knobs, put it in a spritz bottle and spray it in the air as a mist. Use this before difficult discussions that may spark arguments or after a fight.

**please note that you must have a special spoon, cooking pot, and strainer for this potion- this has to be a separate one from everyday culinary use! **

Items Needed:

- A bottle (glass is preferred, you can get a canning jar at a local craft store for under $5.00)
- 1& 1/2 cups Spring Water
- apple cider vinegar or vodka about 1/2 cup*you only need one*
- Lavender herb (handful 1/4 cup) or essential oil (10-20 drops)
- Lemon Verbena herb (handful 1/4 cup) or oil (10-20 drops)
- Sage Leaves (handful 1/4 cup) or oil (5-10 drops)
- 2 whole Star Anise
- 1 whole cinnamon stick
- pot used exclusively for making potions (you can get one cheap at a consignment shop or thrift store- I got mine for .90 cents)
- A wooden spoon you use exclusively for potion making.
- Stove or Campfire. (wood and matches if you choose to make a fire outside)

- Strainer used exclusively for magick.

Timing: The timing for making this potion should be new to full moon.

Prepare yourself as you see fit beforehand (this could include a ritual bath with salt or smudging yourself with burning sage or smokeless sage spray.) Prepare your space by getting the cooking pot, spoon and measured water. Add the water into the saucepan and add in the herbs or oils bring the mixture to a rolling boil then turn down the heat to a low simmer. Stirring the potion in a clockwise manner chant the following several times:

Water & herbs mixed; a potion is formed

Bad energy & anger will be transformed

Peace & tranquility creates a powerful brew

Restoring my home anew.

When you feel this potion is complete (about 30 minutes on a low simmer) strain the mixture into the jar let it cool a bit and then add in the vodka or apple cider vinegar. This potion should last for 30 days if not longer, keep it in a dark cool place, out of direct sunlight. Be sure to make sure you are not allergic to any of the items because they will come in contact with your skin. You can do a test patch in a small hidden spot on your body to make sure there is no reaction before using this product around the house- this is not a BATH and should not be used as such it's just meant as a wash. Washes are a popular practice in the magickal practice of hoodoo.

Health Spells

A Health Spell

Winter can bring about a cold or illness in the blink of an eye. Use this spell to keep yourself healthy and if you do begin to feel the effects of a sickness do it immediately.

this spell should NEVER take the place of visiting a clinic, doctor, hospital, primary care physician. Make sure you are safe to consume the following ingredients

Items Needed:

- Fresh ginger root (a medium sized piece will be okay)
- A ginger grater.
- Honey
- Lemon- probably a bag of lemons because this spell should be repeated often
- Water
- tea cup or mug
- Tea Pot

Timing: Whenever you begin to feel sick or are battling an illness.

Prepare your kitchen area for magick. Begin by grating the ginger and setting it aside you only need a little bit- no more than ⅓ a teaspoon. Slice the lemon into wedges and put it inside the teacup, take the water and begin to boil it within the teapot. As it boils you can use this or a similar chant.

Water toil and water simmer

makes the magick sparkle &
glimmer

infuse this spell with energy and
vigor

to make the magick energy grow
bigger

When the water has boiled pour it over the lemon wedges, let it seep for 3-4 minutes. Stirring in honey in a clockwise motion repeat these or similar words:

Tea made from honey and gold

helps me to fight this awful cold

with each moment I grow
stronger and more like me

as I will it so mote it be!

Stir in the grated ginger and remove the lemons if you wish. Sip at this tea. Throw away lemon remains or compost. Do not use the same lemon for more than one batch of tea. Repeat this spell as often as you desire.

A Healing Chant

This chant is for general healing, it can be combined with other things like candle magick, a healing bath, herbal teas, etc.

Illness visits I am not well

but the time has come to bid it farewell

the Goddess of healing,
Artemis* I hail

good health, and energy will now prevail.

Destroy the sickness, destroy the germs.

I will it to happen and on my terms

I wish to be better _____ night (insert a day)

laughing and enjoying & being alright

By the power of three times three

as I will it so mote it be!

A Healing Spell for a Serious Illness

YOU MUST CONSULT A LICENSED HEALTH PRACTITIONER IN ADDITION TO WORKING THIS SPELL

This spell is to be done for someone who has a serious illness such as: cancer, aids, or another illness. This spell is meant to increase the odds of healing but if it is that person's time it will help them go in a peaceful and dignified way.

Items Needed:

- A Reddish Orange candle
- Matches
- A throw blanket or Scarf- this can be something you make yourself while you focus on the healing of your loved one or something that you purchase and cleanse for the recipient.
- 1 Sunstone crystal
- 1 Celestite crystal
- 1 Smokey Quartz crystal
- Spring water enough to fill the larger bowl to the 1/4- 1/2 mark.
- Two see through glass bowls one smaller than the other. (must be clean) (Pyrex is acceptable)
- Cheese cloth (easily obtained at the supermarket.)

Timing: new moon to full moon. Though if the need is serious anytime will do.

This spell is two parts, the first thing we are going to do is make a crystal potion. Those of you familiar with cooking will understand this concept rather quickly others may not. Taking the large bowl place, it on the countertop, place the smaller bowl inside, there should be a gap between the larger and smaller bowl enough to place inside some spring water being sure that you do not get any inside the smaller bowl. Add your cleansed crystals into the smaller bowl. Cover this set-up with the cheese cloth. Place in the sunlight or moonlight for 3 hours.

When 3 hours has passed you can take the smaller bowl out of the larger one allowing the water to drip into the larger bowl so nothing is wasted.

Watch this video to learn how to make elixirs:

https://www.youtube.com/watch?v=Qyt3qf6xye0

The Above is an example of how to do the double boiler method of crystal Elixirs- specifically the set-up at 2:25 for the black tourmaline)

Light the candle with these or similar words:

Fiery candle of orange and red

empower my spell far ahead

___ is in need of healing and

peace

wellbeing and vitality now

increase

Taking the crystal potion sprinkle it on the blanket or scarf. See the energies of the crystals entering into the fibers of the fabric, you can empower this with these or similar words:

Crystals formed from pressure

and heat

magickal properties my needs

you meet

___ needs energy, healing, and

divine aid

This spell is set, magick made.

Set the magickal water still in the bowl on top of the scarf/blanket and place in front of the candle- allow the candle to burn out safely. When the candle has burn out bury the candle in the ground and water the candle remains with the crystal elixir. Let the garment dry (it will be damp from you sprinkling it with crystal water), write a heartfelt letter to the recipient and then give it to him or her when you go to see them next. Tell them it's blessed with prayers and well wishes and they should wear it whenever they feel they need some extra TLC (tender loving care).

Herbal Spell bottle for Health

Items Needed:

- A blue candle
- A personal item from each person to be kept in good health
- A piece of clear quartz
- Matches
- Inscribing tool
- Eucalyptus Leaves
- Rosemary

- Vervain
- Heal All (herb)
- Mugwort
- Allspice
- A bowl to mix herbs inside
- Funnel

Gather all the ingredients in front of you. Light your blue candle with the intention of creating a magical object to heal and bring healing energies into your home!

Put the bowl in front of you pick up each herb separately and hold them in your hands empowering them, by telling each herb what it's job is within your magick. Place to herbs inside the bowl, it may be necessary to break up some herbs into smaller pieces, for this use your mortar and pestle.

Funnel the herbs inside the bottle.

Pick up the piece of clear quartz and hold it in your projective hand (the one you right with). Tell this clear quartz its job is to bring healing energy to all those infused inside this bottle.

Next add in the taglocks or personal effects inside the bottle stating:

> *(name) good health will come to you (me, them, us)*
>
> *Through this simple healing brew*
>
> *As long as this bottle stays strong*
>
> *Healing for your (my, their, our) whole life long*

Cap the bottle and seal it with the burning candle wax, inscribe upon it healing symbols!

A Simple Spell for Self-Healing

So maybe you have come down with a cold or are just starting to feel a bit out of whack do this spell to help get you back on your A game!

******MEDICAL DISCLAIMER- I am NOT a doctor, if you are sick you MUST go see a licensed medical professional either through your regular practice or the ER/Hospital!
****

Items Needed:

- Bathtub filled with hot water (a bit hotter than you want because it will cool a bit before you get inside).

- One Chamomile Tea bag. (or tied muslin bag with 3 teaspoons of Chamomile herb inside).

- One white Candle.

- Matches

- Inscribing tool.

Timing: Whenever you are sick or getting sick but it's best to do this from full to dark moon. (do this before bed or a nap). Taking the candle and inscribing tool mark your symptoms with a line through it like below:

Ear-ache, Sore Throat.

Run yourself a nice warm bath and light the candle says these or similar words:

Candle burning true and bright

Shedding healing warm light

As you shine upon me

infuse me with your energy.

After the candle is empowered, set it somewhere that it is safe. Next pick up the bag of Chamomile (Tea or Satchel you have made) and dip it into the water swirling it in a clockwise motion softly and methodically- if the water is too hot do not dip your fingers inside. You can intone these or similar words.

Powerful Herb of calm and sleep

Your magickal powers in this water do steep

Let me relax and my body renew

helping me to become like new.

When the water is cool enough for you to get in, remove your clothing and soak in the tub until it gets cool, then submerge yourself or sprinkle yourself with water (for some getting all the way under the water is not possible- especially if you have an ear condition!) Stand up and let the water drain out while saying:

My illness has come and now it goes

stuck in the water I now dispose

down the drain forever gone

Starting now I am me

Strong, energetic, and healthy.

Get out of the water, blow out the candle, wrap yourself up in a towel, and walk out of the bathroom do not go back into the bathroom until you are sure ALL the water is out of the tub this is important you cannot look back at the water you are leaving behind. Technically no one else in the family should go in either until the water is all gone. When you are dressed get into bed and go to sleep while you are relaxed. When you wake up remove the candle from your property or save the candle for later if you plan to repeat this spell several times until you get 100%

VARIATION FOR THOSE WHO CAN'T TAKE A BATH

Items Needed:

- Pitcher with HOT water.
- One Chamomile Tea bag. (or tied muslin bag with 3 teaspoons of Chamomile herb inside).
- One white Candle.
- Matches
- Inscribing tool.

Timing: Whenever you are sick or getting sick but it's best to do this from full to dark moon. (do this before bed or a nap)

Taking the candle and inscribing tool mark your symptoms with a line through it like below:

Ear-ache, Sore Throat.

Fill the pitcher with water and light the candle say these or similar words:

Candle burning true and bright

Shedding healing warm light

As you shine upon me

infuse me with your energy.

After the candle is empowered, set it somewhere that it is safe. Next pick up the bag of Chamomile (Tea or Satchel you have made) and dip it into the water swirling it in a clockwise motion softly and methodically- if the water is too hot do not dip your fingers inside. You can intone these or similar words.

Powerful Herb of calm and sleep

Your magickal powers in this

water do steep

Let me relax and my body

renew

helping me to become like new.

When the water is cool enough for you place this inside the shower, remove your clothing and start the shower running; get inside and wash your body as you normally do, then pouring the water from the pitcher SLOWLY OVER YOUR HEAD say:

My illness has come and now it

goes

stuck in the water I now dispose

down the drain forever gone

Starting now I am me

Strong, energetic, and healthy.

Turn off the shower, Get out, blow out the candle, wrap yourself up in a towel, and walk out of the bathroom do not go back into the bathroom until you are sure ALL the water is out of the shower this is important you cannot look back at the water you are leaving behind. Technically no one else in the family should go in either until the water is all gone. When you are dressed get into bed and go to sleep while you are relaxed. When you wake up remove the candle from your property or save the candle for later if you plan to repeat this spell several times until you get 100%

Love Spells

A Charm Bag for Love

Items needed:

- A square of red/pink cloth (or a pre-made mojo bag)

- A piece of Pink or red ribbon or yarn

- Basil

- Rose petals (pink or red being best)
- rose quartz
- Rhodochrosite
- a piece of paper with the words "Love come to me" written upon it- preferably in pink or red ink.
- pink or red candle
- a pin or inscribing tool
- an oil appropriate to the working of love-such as; rose oil, come to me oil, love me oil, basil oil.

Gather your ingredients; lay out the piece of fabric in the center of your working space. Take the candle and carve upon it your desire for love, write down anything you find to be important. Anoint the candle with the oil stroking the candle towards the wick while thinking of drawing your love to you. Light the candle with these words:

I call across land and sea

For my true love to come to me

Pick up the herbs you are using and hold them in your hand. Visualize a special love coming into your life. Repeat the phrase above

I call across land and sea

For my true love to come to me

Next pick up the crystals you are using and connect with their helper spirit. Tell the spirit what you wish to accomplish. Place your stones on the fabric while repeating:

I call across land and sea

For my true love to come to me

Take the piece of paper written upon it the words "Love come to me" Take your candle and drip wax around those words in the shape of a heart. Hold the paper in your hands after the wax has cooled and speak to it your desires breath upon it the very breath of your goal. Take the oil and anoint around the inside border of the wax heart.

Fold the paper towards you in a multiple of three (3,6,9, or 12…).

Allow the candle to burn out completely and take the fabric and form a bag (or add the ingredients inside the pre-made bag) being sure to add in any cooled (unlit) candle remains. Take your yarn or ribbon and tie it around the bundle in a multiple of three (let spirit move you to which number) while reciting these words:

This charm is made the spell is cast

Bring me my lover and bring (him/her) fast!

Then place the bag under your pillow at night and in your pocket or purse during the day, feel it often imaging your love coming to you!

See Me Spell

One of my readers emailed me about a situation he is in and would like a special someone to notice him. While my advice is twofold magick and mundane, here is the spell. After you do the spell dear reader(s), be sure you get the guts and walk up to the object of your affection and initiate things. If this spell bothers your ethics, do not do it- certainly there is no one telling you that you must- or just adapt it.

Items Needed:

- Red Candle
- Inscribing Tool
- Matches
- Piece of Paper
- Pen
- Fireproof Dish
- A piece of fruit as an offering to Aphrodite

Timing: Waxing to Full Moon

Gather the required items and prepare yourself as you normally do for magick. Inscribe the persons name and birthday who you wish to notice you. If you do not know their birthday, I recommend a web search Facebook + Twitter + Myspace gives us all sorts of juicy witchy details for magickutilize the resources you have available. Light the candle with these words:

Aphrodite Goddess of love and desire

empower my spell and light the fire

I want ___ to see me now

empower me to dazzle and wow!

Take the piece of paper and write down what you wish to happen "I want ___ to look favorably upon my request for a date." or something along those lines, fold the paper towards you 9 times, and then set it afire while saying these words:

The fire consumed my spell I am set

I know that with Aphrodite my

needs are met

___ will see what I have to

share

and what I have is beyond

compare.

Let the candle burn and the ashes cool, take the remains of this spell and the piece of fruit outside to a wooded space and leave as an offering. Do not forget now you must make plans and ask this person out or over for dinner or something- remember though that no matter what NO means NO- respect this person's wishes and rework the spell and try again. Gentleman get ladies, and ladies get MEN. If you mess with someone else's mate, you can expect that it will happen to you. Play the game but play it nice.

Aphrodite Love Spell

In this spell we are going to be working with the Goddess of Love Aphrodite.

Items Needed:

- A Scallop Shell
- A Pink Candle
- A Sweet-smelling oil or perfume
- Matches
- Candle Holder

Timing: Waxing moon, full moon, rising tide, high tide, Valentine's day.

Gather the required ingredients and prepare yourself as you normally would for magick. When you are ready, light the candle with this incantation:

> *Great Aphrodite who rides free*
> *on the sea foam*
>
> *Bring love to me as your long*
> *golden locks you comb*
>
> *Help me to enchant all those*
> *that I see*

bringing the perfect lover right

to me.

Next take the scallop shell and pass it over the candle flame, begin to empower this shell. See the type of lover you wish to bring into your life. Take some of your sweet-smelling perfume/oil and anoint the shell. You can say these or similar words:

Shell sacred to the Goddess of

Love

draw in a mate who fits me like

a glove

let our match be seamless and

right

perfect talks and passionate at

night

let him come without delay

give me the guidance to meet

him halfway.

May in no way this spell reverse

or place upon me any curse

Let the candle burn out; you may wish to gently poke a hole in the base of the shell and wear it as a talisman.

A Love Chant

Use this chant to increase your love; this can be used in spells to find new love as well.

Pink and Red the colors of

yearning

increase the passion make it

burning

blocks removed that keep me

from my desire

a great passionate love I do

now acquire.

A New Year's Eve Love Spell

Let's work some magick to find love in the new year!

Items Needed:

- A Pink Rose
- A white or pink candle in a holder
- matches
- Rose Quartz
- A Glass of Water
- a mojo bag of your choice (red/pink/white- would be good!)

Timing: New Year's Eve

For this spell gather your required ingredients and prepare yourself as you normally would for magick. Light the pink candle using these or similar words:

> *candle burns bright into the night*
>
> *to help increase my magick sight*
>
> *out there is a love for me*
>
> *with this candle him/her I can now see*

Holding the rose in your hand starting at the bottom of your feet work your way up to your head directing energy through the rose into your body use these or similar words:

> *Flower of love flower of emotion*

help bring love to me with
forward motion

infuse my soul, body and my
mind

so great love is something I can
find

Holding the water in your hands swirl it gently in a clockwise (building) motion (in the southern hemisphere perhaps counterclockwise is the building direction). Chant the following:

I open myself to lasting
romance

may we know each other at first
glance

When the power has built as high as it will go drink 3/4 of the water saving a bit for a libation (or offering) outside. Let the candle burn out. Afterwards, place the rose petals, rose quartz, and a dab of the water in a mojo bag which you should carry with you all of 2014. Place the stem & water outside as an offering to the divine powers.

MAY LOVE FIND YOU!

A Soulmate Love Chant

Are you looking for Soulmate love to come your way? Try this chant. You can add in pink or red candles, rose quartz, rhodochrosite, rhodonite, etc. The scents of Rose, jasmine, and sandalwood inspire love and lust.

My love is out there we have yet

to meet

I want our love to be strong yet

sweet

physically, emotionally, and

spiritually akin*

my other half, my soul, my twin.

the barriers that keep us apart

now dissolve and depart

Together in no time we will be

as I will it so mote it be!

*Akin: having similar characteristics, properties, etc. (source)

A Spell Bottle for Love

Items Needed:

- Rose Petals
- Jasmine flower petals (substitute pansy flowers)
- Lavender
- Rose quartz stone
- A sprig of Ivy

- Medium to Large Bottle
- Pink Candle (or Red)
- A dash of fresh nutmeg
- A bowl for mixing ingredients
- A funnel for sifting ingredients into the bottle
- Inscribing tool
- Matches/Lighter

Gather your ingredients in front of you. Light the candle and declare magick is about to take place either by casting a circle or making a statement of intent.

Hold the rose petals in your hand feel them with your fingers are they soft and silky or dry and crunchy? Smell them, do they have a fragrance? Tell the rose petals what you desire them to do for you, in your own words. When you feel this is complete add them to the bowl.

Take the jasmine flowers in your hands; I personally love the smell of real jasmine, empower this herb to bring to you the love you desire! When you are ready add this herb to the bowl

Ivy has long been used as a plant to bind in love. Adding in this plant will help you bind the love you desire to you. Hold this plant in your hands and ask it to bind to you a love true and strong. When you are ready add this plant into the bowl.

Nutmeg is used to ensure fidelity in a relationship, if this is not something you want in a loving relationship then omit this herb. However, if you would like to ensure your lover will be faithful to you, then put a dash of this spice in your hands and empower it to bring you a lover with only eyes for you. Add it to the bowl when finished.

Sit for a moment and concentrate on your goal of finding and keeping a love that is meant for you. When you have an image firmly placed in your mind run your fingers through the herbal mixture in your bowl empowering it even further to assist you in your goal. You may want to add a chant at this time such as:

I call across land and sea

For my true love to come to me

You then should drip a couple of drops of wax from your candle to the herbal mixture empowering it with the element of fire to bring you this special love.

Take the funnel and pour the mixture into the bottle. Please note the ivy leaves unless broken up may not fit into the bottle without rolling them up and stuffing them inside- I suggest this is done at the end, so just remove them as you come across them in the funnel process.

Once the herbs and ivy are added into the bottle take your rose quartz stone and hold it in your projective hand. Empower this magickal crystal with the power of love to bring you the best love for you right now in your life.

-:- -:- -:-

You can also add in a slip of paper with your goals written upon it, it is up you as a responsible witch if you want to add any person effects (taglocks) of a specific individual inside this bottle- I cannot tell you whether or not that is something you should do- only YOU can decide if that is something that just HAS to be done.

Take your finished bottle and drip wax from the candle all around the mouth and the lid (cork/or cap) to make a seal, you can then etch into this a love symbol such as a heart or the Venus and mars symbols

This bottle is meant to be kept near your bed, you can put it on top of a dresser, vanity, bedside table, under your bed… you decide where this potent magickal love bottle will be kept!

Don't forget to pick it up and send loving thoughts to it to strengthen your magick!

<u>Love Spell</u>

<u>Required items</u>:

- A Rose Quartz Crystal
- Pink Pen
- Paper
- White or Pink Candle
- Matches
- Rose incense or Rose Essential Oil (you can use fragrance oil here)
- Small pink bag

Timing: New to Full Moon

Set aside an hour or so that you will be undisturbed, gather your required items. Prepare yourself as you normally do for magick, this could be a bath or maybe you will smudge yourself with incense.

When you are ready light the candle and begin to focus on what it is you desire right now in your life. Think about how you are worthy of the love and relationship that you desire the most. Pick up the rose quartz pass it through the incense or place a small dab of the rose oil and hold it in front of the candle saying the following:

Crystal of Pink and White

I charge you with this candle light

Bring to me the love I ask

Now you have your magickal task

Set the stone down and take up the pen and paper and begin to write down what it is you truly want. When you have finished this hold the rose quartz in your left hand and your paper in the right- read out the paper and imagine a person coming into your life. Do not see a particular person- this would be unethical (and not because of Harm None). Place the crystal down and fold the paper 4 times each time towards you- you are bringing this into your life.

Place the paper down in front of the candle and place the stone on top saying the following:

I call to me love

charged by the rose quartz above

I know I deserve the best

Just as I wrote, I do request

As I will it, so mote it be

By the power of three times three

The Spell is done. Let the candle burn out; when everything is cooled place the items in a pink bag and either carry it with you or place it under your pillow.

Protection Spells

Banishing Incense

Use this magickal blend to help get rid of the nasties that may be inhabiting your space!

Ingredients:

- Frankincense
- Sandalwood
- Sage
- A pinch of salt
- a black tourmaline stone or chip.

These ingredients when mixed together will bring about a total shift in the atmosphere of a place! Mix the ingredients together adding the crystal last. Hold the black tourmaline crystal in your hand seeing it as a vacuum cleaner meant to suck up all the nasty energy all around you. The tourmaline is not meant to be burnt on a charcoal block but used to empower the mixture!

A Spell to Break Ties

I am going through something in my personal life which requires me breaking and severing some ties that I have had in place for a long time. These ties served me for a long time but they are no longer serving me and I feel it is best for me to cut and release. What you read is the spell I'll be performing.

Items Needed:

- Black candle
- A white candle
- a piece of string or cord
- a pair of scissors
- inscribing tool
- matches
- candle holder

- two razor shells
- a picture representation of me and the person I'll be separating from.

Timing: Waning to Dark moon.

Tide: High to Low Tide.

Gather the required items and prepare yourself for magic, cleanse yourself and your working space with whatever method you find is best. Inscribe your name on the top part of the candle and then draw a line and then write whatever you wish to break ties with if it's a person write their name if it's an addiction or thing write its name. You can also draw pictures.

When the candle is ready place it within the holder, arrange the pictures or representations on either side of your space place the razor shells in between you and the item, with the string connecting both. On your-side place the white candle, on the other items side place the black candle.

When you are ready light the black candle with this incantation:

Our time together is now complete

our hold on each other will be obsolete

I no longer will affect you

your power on me I also undo

Unless our paths are meant to be

This is my final goodbye to thee

May in no way this spell reverse

or place upon me any curse.

As I will it so mote it be!

In about fifteen minutes cut the cord between you and the other representation lighting the white candle with the same incantation. Let both candles burn out, the white should finish last. When the spell is complete remove all remains including the physical representations from your house. You can cleanse the shells, the candle stick, the scissors, and inscribing tool, everything else should be thrown away.

This spell may need to be repeated- trust your instincts.

Return to Sender Spell

We all have times when we are dealing with some bad energy and think it may be from that person who just won't leave us alone- maybe we don't even know who it is! Use this spell to remove their energy from your life and send it right on back to them!

Items Needed:

- A mirror (this needs to be able to stand up or be propped up).

- A Black Candle

- A White candle

- Long Matches or extended lighter.

- Inscribing Tool

- Salt

- Hyssop Herb

Timing: Waning Moon, Saturday.

There are quite a few items in this spell, you may need to start collecting several days before. When you are ready, prepare yourself and your space for magick. The lay out of this spell is important I'll try to explain it the best I can. Taking the black candle be sure that it's light will be reflected in the mirror- but the white candle will not.

Also, the reflection should not ever capture your body once the black candle is lit- so long matches may be needed. The idea is the black candle will capture the harmful energy and reflect it out into the cosmos and therefore the wrong-doer, if it captures your essence it will then reflect it back to you- causing no change to manifest for you.

Taking the black candle inscribe your name upon its surface and a line through the words 'harmful energies'- if you know the sender write their name too. Place the candle in its holder and position the mirror as detailed above. Carefully light the candle while intoning these or similar words:

Creature of fire set in black,

negative energy and psychic attack.

All the harm sent my way,

Shall be returned without delay.

Taking the white candle inscribe your name with the words "positive energy, love, happiness, abundance." Position this candle so it's light baths you but is NOT reflected in the mirror. As you light the candle intone these or similar words:

White light brings a new birth

with great abundance and mirth

I welcome in the energy of love

blessed by the God & Goddess above.

Taking the hyssop and salt mix them together best you can- infusing them with positive energy- sprinkle the mixture between the two candles including the mirror as a barrier.

Know that the energies are being sent back and new more positive ones will take its place.

A Protection Chant

Do you feel like you need some extra protection? This chant will help you feel at peace. If you are in harm's way or in immediate danger, work this as you go to local authorities who are trained to protect you.

Protective bubble of silver light

Guards me both day and night

I am protected from harm

by the power of this little charm

Spirit or person are no test

for this spell keeps me blessed.

Safe & protected I shall be

*by the power of three times
three*

A Weather Protection Spell

As the winter season approaches weather can take a turn for the worse very fast. This is especially prevalent as a Nor'easter heads towards the east coast right in time for Thanksgiving. This spell can be adapted for any weather situation or potential natural disaster.

Items Needed:

- A Small drawstring bag. (I would choose black but you can use whatever you have on hand.)

- A Black stone (I would use either hematite/tourmaline/or any stone found outside that calls to you)

- Olive Oil

- Salt (just a pinch.)

- A small mixing vessel. (a shot glass works well here.)
- Piece of paper
- Pen
- A White or Black Candle with a holder.
- Matches

Timing: Whenever needed- especially potent though Saturday.

Gather the required items and arrange them in a way that is aesthetically pleasing to your working space. Prepare yourself as you normally do for magick and light the candle. You can intone the main chant for this spell as you light the candle if you wish.

Fill the small vessel with olive oil ¾ of the way. Add in a pinch of salt and stir it up- you can use the tip of your athame, wand, pointer finger, whatever works for you. Mix this potion in a counter-clockwise direction three times, then a clockwise direction three time.

Place a dab of this potion on your finger, looking at the potion begin to empower it by sending energy to it. Dip your finger back into the potion and stir again clockwise three times.

Take a dab and place it on the rock, anoint the rock.

Bad weather is headed my way

Protection from Rain and snow
I pray

Make me and those I care about
secure

defense to life and property
insure

In a protective space we shall
be

As I will it so mote it be.

When the stone has been anointed you can place it within the bag. Then take the piece of paper and write out the situation; if snow is coming write down "protection from snow/blizzard", if it's a severe thunderstorm write "protection from thunderstorm and tornado." anoint the paper with the potion and fold the paper towards you.

Place the paper in the bag, secure the bag, and you can place it within your pocket or purse if you must go out or travel. Or this bag can be placed in the center of your house/property if you are going to be home.

The idea of the spell is not to make a storm go away, but to make sure that the worst does not affect you. Perhaps you will get less snow or your power will remain on while others goes out.

Working magick to dismantle a storm is a bad idea it has wide ranging effects on the entire planet. I always recommend working magick for protection during natures various weather patterns/natural disasters.

A Spell to Sever Tires

Today; I woke up and felt the need to severe the ties from some destructive people in my life. Join me as I cast this spell to remove people who are causing you harm or getting rid of other things that need to go.

Items Needed:

- Salt (a decent amount).

- A mirror
- A Black or Navy-blue candle in a cheap disposable candle holder
- An inscribing tool
- Matches
- Holly Leaves

Timing: Waning Moon (full- dark).

Gather your items and prepare yourself as you normally do for spell work, take your inscribing tool and carve the candle with the things you wish to "sever" the ties with.

This can be a habit, a person, an object etc. In the middle of your working space, place the mirror around the mirror draw a circle of salt around that, on top of the mirror place the holly leaves and the candle in the center. The candle will burn and remove all emotional attachments negative energy and the salt will keep the outside safe.

The holly leaves are a protective leaf and can also "return to sender" so if anyone is wishing you harm this set up will help with that as well. I will be intoning these words, you can use them or something similar:

A candle to burns ___ away

from my soul

I take back my power I take

back control

you were sly and sneaky a slimy

snake

but your words were poison and

your smiles fake

I sever the ties that tied us, I am

unbound

by the sky above and the solid

ground

in no way will this spell reverse,

or place upon me any curse

Let the candle burn out to nothing; remove all objects (candle remains/holder/leaves/mirror etc.)

from your property do not turn back. If you cannot throw away these items; immediately wash all the remains and items with a mixture of salt water and rosemary, then a cold-water rinse. Let them have one lunar cycle to recharge from this working.

A Spell to Rid Yourself of Someone Who Needs to Go

There will be times in your life when you will need to bid farewell to someone who has overstayed their welcome or was never welcomed in the first place but inserted themselves into your life. This spell moves that person a long by giving them something better to focus on! In some ways this spell may break "Harm None" depending on how "strict" you follow that "guideline."

Items Needed:

- A brown/navy blue/white candle- pick the color you have on hand
- matches
- inscribing tool
- sheet of aluminum foil

Timing- though this spell would work best during a waning moon you can do this whenever the need is great.

For this spell inscribe the person's name on the candle and draw a line through their name. Prepare yourself and your space and hold the candle in your hand. Imagine yourself getting the news that this person has moved on to better things and are on their way far from you. Place the candle to burn on the aluminum foil & light it with these or similar words:

The time has come to go our separate way

the time is now there can be no delay

you have overstayed your welcome in my life

you have caused me too much strife

as this candle burns away

something more appealing

comes your way

You won't stay to bother me

Because now you're free!

Let the candle burn until it goes out on its own wrap the remains in the aluminum foil and remove immediately from your property, this can be thrown away at a public trash can or taken deep within the woods and buried. Do not look back once you throw the item away, otherwise it could "follow you back". Repeat this spell as needed.

A Traditional Witches' Protection Bottle

This is my take on a traditional Witches Bottle!

Ingredients needed:

- Broken glass
- Nails

- Pins
- Broken mirror- if you already have it
- A sterilized needle
- A funnel
- Rosemary
- Solomon's Seal herb
- Mandrake
- Black Candle
- Inscribing tool
- Matches/lighter
- A bowl set aside for magick only

Gather your ingredients in one centralized location, a working table or other area. It is up to you if you desire to cast a circle if you do however, please ensure that you have a cup or vial of your urine inside the working space as this is a key ingredient to this spell! Otherwise if you do not cast a circle you can obtain this during the process.

Light your candle and declare your purpose.

Inside the jar add in your nails, glass, mirror bits, and pins.

In a dedicated magickal bowl (because poisonous ingredients will be added- this is not a bowl you want to ever eat out of again) add in your mandrake, rosemary, and Solomon's seal herb. Hold your hands over the herb (not in the herbal mixture) and see your essence meshing with that of the herbal mixture. Tell these herbs that you need them to protect you from physical, mental, magickal, and psychic harm. Blend your essences together and when you feel the time has come then add them into the bottle.

Once the herbs and pins, broken glass, nails, and a broken mirror have been added then it is time to fill the bottle almost to the top (about ¼ of an inch to the top) with urine. You can pee in a cup and funnel it into your bottle or just try to get it all in the bottle- personally I think it would be easier to urinate inside the cup and funnel it into a bottle. If you do decide to just urinate in the bottle be sure that no body parts touch the outer edge of the bottle where any of the poisonous herbs may have touched!!!

Before you cap this bottle take the sterilized needle (easily found at a pharmacy) and prick your finger and add in a drop of your blood to this mixture. The goal is to tie this mixture to you 100%.

Cap the bottle and seal tight with drippings from the black candle adding fire energy (strength) to your magick!

Carve protective symbols into the warm wax to seal the process.

-:- -:- -:-

This jar is meant to be put somewhere as close to the front door as possible and in a hidden space, the back of a cabinet, a closet, buried next to your front door? Only you know the lay out of your house/apartment.

Protection and Banishing Jar

This is not so much a spell as it a magickal tool!

Items Needed:

- A large Jar
- Aluminum Foil
- Glue (I used rubber cement)
- Several Sheets of Paper(optional)

- Black Marker
- Ideas of some magickal symbols for protection

Actions:

Gather your items into one place. Cover outside of the jar with aluminum foil shiniest side facing inward. Draw or paste protective symbols on the outside.

Inside goes all your fears, doubts, and worries. On the dark of the moon take the contents in the jar and burn them during a banishing ritual.

Make sure that the foil covering the outside stays in place any open space where you can see what is inside the jar or the glass will cause those fears, doubts, and worries to affect you. If anything does happen to the jar that would compromise its magick dispose of it off your property and make another one!

A Banishing Spell

Items Needed:

- Citrine stone
- Hematite stone

- Slip of paper with things you want to banish written
- Black candle
- Matches
- Screw or another inscribing tool
- A white candle
- Matches
- Fire proof container
- tweezers

<u>The Actions</u>:

Take the black candle and inscribe upon it the things you wish to banish or the things written on your paper so keep it to bullet points- use your inscribing tool- I used a screw.

Assemble all items on a surface such as an altar or table or ground if performing outside

Cast your circle

Call on the forces you wish to call on- elements- Goddess/God

State the things you wish to banish and light the black candle- speak out-loud again the things you wish to banish- push them into the candle flame (mentally)

Take the slip of paper hold it in your hands take some bodily fluid (spit or blood whatever you're comfortable with) anoint the paper – read it out-loud and set it afire.

Insure it all burns- you can use a pair of tweezers to do this.

Hold the hematite in your projective hand and citrine in your right state:

citrine to bring in the positive

bright energy

hematite to suck out the things

that I banish

Hold them tight until it either

hurts to do so- or you feel it all

has been completed.

Put them down; take the white candle and light it from the black say:

there is light in this darkness it will shine

positive light into the future

Make a pyramid shape from your hands and hold it in front of the black candle so the flame is in the center imagine again the bad things you wish to banish being pushed out through your palms While chanting

I banish you

you are gone from my life

Clap your hands when you reach the peak of chanting.

Move now to the white candle imagine drawing in the energies that will help you move past that which must be banished. Do not clap draw your hands to your body (where-ever you feel your hands must go)

Let the black and white candle burn as the black burns banishing takes place and white represents illumination and positive energies! – thank the things you called- Close the circle.

Sea Witchery

A Sea Witch Harassment Chant

***LEGAL DISCLAIMER-

if you are in danger of your life or property call the proper local authorities right away- this chant is to be used in combination with regular methods of safety***

Use this chant to help protect you from being harassed. You can use it mentally when you see someone approaching you, if you feel you are in danger, or to stop someone from stalking you.

fishing hook captures the fish

bring to me my little wish

it's time for ___ to go far away

I am no longer your prey.

I am free from your abuse

stalking, lying, and misuse.

You can no longer bother me

as I will it so mote it be!

A Sea Witch Protection Chant

This is a Sea-Witch protection chant. A personal favorite of mine.

lobster claw and fishes scale

icy rain and oceans gale

sweep me up in a protective space

keep me safe in your murky

embrace

Use this chant when you feel you are in danger and need protection. You can walk around the perimeter of your house while saying this chant, during the summer if you find some crab shells you can powder them up and add in some salt and sprinkle it around your property.

A Sea Witch Self Love Spell

As we approach valentine's day, the most important love spell we can cast is one on ourselves. If we do not love and value ourselves and our happiness, no one else will.

Items Needed:

- A Treat for yourself- you pick this could be edible, a new book, a movie, a bubble bath etc.

- One Rose

- Your Sea Witch Candle.

- Matches

Timing: Waxing Moon- Full moon, valentine's day.

Tide: Rising to high tide.

Place your treat to yourself in front of you, if it's something like a bubble bath or perhaps a trip to the coolest local place, then just stand in front of it or have it in your line of vision. Light your Sea Witch Candle with the given invocation:

Undines element of water, ruler

of the sea

come and lend your energies to

me

there is magick to be done

aid my working my spells begun

State your purpose for this magickal working, "to show myself self-love and care, that I am worth it in every-way." Repeat this verse while you hold the rose:

Circles and spirals the water goes

A special gift plus an enchanted rose

I love myself through good and bad it's true

I deserve the best a major breakthrough!

May I see what does me wrong

So, I am free safe from harm

A simple act of self-love I am set

I promise myself all my needs will be met.

When you have said that, tuck that rose somewhere special, perhaps you can keep it with you if not place it aside and set it in a place of prominence later. Go do your act of self-love. Remember to check in with yourself and make sure you are truly happy. This spell can be repeated as needed, it does not have to be valentine's day. Anytime the moon is growing or the tide is rising, this spell can be done. When you are finished you can blow out your Sea Witch Candle.

A Sea Witch Charm Empowerment Chant

I am giving you a chant to empower your charms and tools.

Humpback whale diving deep

set my magick, my goals to reap.

empower my ___ make it strong

help to move my spells along

Moray Eel remove the blocks

from my tools, herbs, and rocks.

lend your help to set my spell

insuring that it all goes well.

Ocean life from crab to fish

I call on your help for my wish.

I give Thanks to you for helping me

As I will it so mote it be!

Ocean Wish Spell

Next time you go to the ocean (or if you are really land locked you can do this spell at home in a bathtub) do this spell to work on a secret wish you have. This spell will be assuming you are at the beach if you cannot you will need to adapt this yourself.

Items Needed:

- A stick

- A found beach treasure such as a shell, a stone, maybe a worn piece of beach glass.

Timing: Waxing Moon to full moon.

Tide: Coming in to high tide.

You will need to create a sigil of what it is you desire. So, if it's money you will need to assign numerical values to each of the letters with this chart:

<u>1</u>	<u>2</u>	<u>3</u>	<u>4</u>	<u>5</u>	<u>6</u>	<u>7</u>	<u>8</u>	<u>9</u>
a	b	c	d	e	f	g	h	i
j	k	l	m	n	o	p	q	r
s	t	u	v	w	x	y	z	

So, let us use love: that would be; 3,6,4,5. next you will need a number square:

4	9	2
3	5	7
8	1	6

So, this number square has been done for a different need it appears it was something like 3,6,4,5. whatever the pattern is that you have gotten that would be your symbol/sigil. so, it appears our sigil may look something like this:

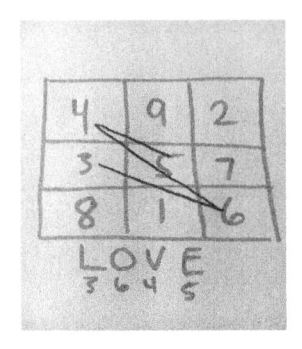

So, with your special sigil for money in hand walk to the water's edge, greet the ocean. Tell it our purpose:

Ocean open and deep

Magick and mystery you keep

I have a need for ___ today

help me to bring it about right away

Draw the symbol in the sand near the incoming water's edge- if it's cold this is a task because you don't want to get wet. If it's warm this could be quite fun getting the entire symbol written while the waves crash at your feet. If you have children get them into this; they do not need to do the sigil work you could let them draw a heart for more friends, or a dollar sign for some extra money. They may even surprise you with their imaginative symbols for what it is they want- there is no wrong drawing. When you have drawn the sigil into the sand step back, give the shell or glass or trinket you found back to the ocean as an offering. If you want a touchstone of your magick find a new shell or beach treasure. Before you leave the beach be sure to say Thank you, in your own special way.

AT HOME ADAPTATION.

We will do the same thing; create a sigil of what it is we need- we may wish to add candles, and incense or whatever else we desire. Take a magick marker (Crayola works well), water color pencils, etc. and a piece of paper and write the sigil down. Repeat the above incantation near the tub or basin of water. The water in your tub was once from the ocean- all water is connected! Take the sigil paper and dip it within the water, watch it bleed and fade away. Give thanks to the water, you may wish to anoint yourself with the water because you want to bring something to you. Let the water go down the drain or pour it outside if you are using a basin. As you let go the water see your magick shooting off to be completed.

extra magick- if you are a reiki 2 practitioner draw the reiki power symbol over top, including the long-distance reiki symbol to send energy to the goal so it can manifest quicker. Reiki masters can draw the reiki master symbol to add extra power.

Sand Dollar Money Spell

We are going to be using the mighty sand dollar to bring us some money for a particular need we may have.

Items Needed:

- Sand dollar
- Small green candle
- candle holder

- matches
- seaweed flakes
- seaweed oil – this can be made by taking an oil and infusing seaweed flakes in it for several days straining the seaweed.
- A piece of paper
- A green pen or pencil.

Timing: Waxing to full

Tide: Rising to high

Gather the required items, you may need to do some prep work several days in advance to make the seaweed oil. To begin with anoint the candle with the seaweed oil and roll the oiled candle in the seaweed flakes, if you can't find seaweed flakes then crush some seaweed sheets to make flakes or a powder. Light the green candle with these words:

Abundance of the ocean and

tide

green candle and seaweed dried

empower my magick make it fly

bring me money in ample supply.

Hold the sand dollar in your hands, the sand dollar is a symbol of the ocean of the pentacle and because it has the name dollar in it, we can use it in abundance and money magick. This once living organism, lived off small edible particles within the sand, it has given its life and we must honor it.

You may wish to say a quick prayer or give it an offering; when you have honored it in some way, empower it to bring you money and abundance:

sand dollar seeker through the grain

help me with my financial gain

I need __ $ to pay what's due

plus, a little extra too.

Help me with this important task

if it wasn't I wouldn't ask.

Empowered by the power of three

as I will it so mote it be!

Place the sand dollar down and write on a piece of paper how much money you need to pay your bills plus a little extra too. Bless it by passing it quickly through the candle flame, and then under the sand dollar. Let the candle burn out. You may want to repeat this spell until the money comes, be open to the abundance, accept any and all small offers for money such as: helping a neighbor, working overtime, giving assistance to someone in need, being observant. Money comes in many ways, so be sure you are not blocking the universes answer to your spell.

A Sea Witch Money Spell

You will need access to some nautically themed ingredients for this spell.

Items Needed:

- Seaweed (fresh is better, but the kind at markets is okay)
- A Mermaid's Purse /skate egg case. (pictured above)
- A Green mojo bag or piece of paper.
- One large coin in your countries denomination.
- A Green Candle
- Matches
- Candle Holder

Timing: Waxing Moon, rising- high tide.

Gather your required ingredients and prepare yourself for magick. Hold the green candle in your hands and enchant it by sending energy towards it while focusing on your goal. I like to use this enchantment for empowering my candles for sea witchery:

Undines element of water, ruler

of the sea

come and lend your energies to

me

there is magick to be done

aid my working my spells begun

When the candle is charged carve a set amount of money into its side and light the candle flame. Then hold your hands over the other ingredients seaweed is an abundant vegetation in the ocean. Send your energy to each item, empowering it for its special purpose. Seaweed, it is a great source of minerals and vitamins and very healthy for you. It brings abundance, you can place the seaweed inside the mojo bag or lay it on the center of the paper. Then hold the mermaids purse, this is actually an egg sack for the skate, hold this in your hands and see the money you have growing and multiplying you can place that within the mojo bag or next to the seaweed on the paper. Finally add the coin.

You can again place your hands over the items on the paper or grasp the bag and hold it within your hands. The time has come to do one final charging before finishing the spell. These are the words that I use:

The ocean provides abundant

life

bring me abundance to end my

strife

water empowers the items

within this bag

enchanted by the mermaid and

sea hag

bring abundant money to me

as I will it so mote it be.

When you have empowered the items, you can tie up your mojo bag, if you are working on the paper packet method begin folding the sides towards you (bring in the money) and rotating clockwise. You can secure the packet with either glue, a piece of tape, or tying it while using knot magick. Place this inside your purse or near your bank books. The spell is done.

A Sea Witch Psychic Chant

Use this chant to bring out your psychic abilities, you can use it before reading Tarot, Runes or scrying.

I call to the ocean deep and ocean wide.

psychic knowledge comes with rising tide,

let me see what I must perceive

A special message I wish to receive

Let this happen without delay

with ocean current and salty bay.

Wealth Spells

A Seaweed Money Spell

Seaweed is found in abundance in the ocean, it also provides some great nutritional benefits for those who consume it.

Items Needed:

- A small boiling saucepan of water
- Edible seaweed (found at the supermarket)
- Beef or Chicken Bouillon cubes.

Timing: Waxing Moon, full moon, rising tide, high tide

This spell is to be done at your stove or hotplate. Boil some water, as the water boils empower it with this verse:

Water heats to a rolling simmer

Magick increases with glitter and shimmer

The heat charges this potion with power

soon this charm I will devour

When the water is at a rapid boil add in one of the bouillon cubes to make a broth, as it dissolves you can repeat the above incantation. Hold your hands over the seaweed and begin to see the green become money, take a sheet and break it into small pieces and begin to add to the boiling broth, saying these or similar words:

seaweed abundant gift of the sea

bringing money and abundance

to me

help to make me healthy and

strong

bringing wellness and riches

along

Take the soup off the stove and let it cool, add pepper or other seasonings to taste. Eat warm. If this soup is too much for you to eat or it does not taste pleasant, think of items that can be added to make it more appealing: carrots, peas, noodles, etc. Save a small amount to give as an offering to a plant or tree outside.

The Spell is done.

Enchanted Pennies

Create enchanted pennies to draw more money towards you.

Items Needed:

- Green Candle
- Candle Stick
- Matches
- Olive Oil
- A handful of Pennies (the more the merrier)
- Cauldron

Timing: Waxing to Full Moon

Tide: Rising to High Tide

Gather the required ingredients for this spell. Set up the working space in a way that is pleasant to you. Prepare yourself for this spell by cleansing and clearing yourself and your space.

Anoint your green candle with the olive oil by working from the end to the top, you can carve money signs and other relevant symbols into the candle as well. Light the candle with words of power:

Money, money comes my way

bringing wealth and abundance

today.

After you have lit the candle, place the pennies into the cauldron- see the money, multiplying within the cauldron, hold the candle over the cauldron and circle the candle in a clockwise manner. You should chant the previous enchantment:

Money, money comes my way

bringing wealth and abundance

today.

When you feel the power raise, place the candle on top of the pennies and let it burn out. Fill your wallet up with the pennies and each time you go out to a store leave a penny, leave it with the knowledge that more will come running back to you. You can give them out as well to people in need.

A Money Chant

Diamonds and silver pot of gold

Bring me the riches I have told

Always abundance and money for play

Let this start to happen today.

Quick Cash Spell

This spell will help bring in some quick money.

Items Needed:

- A Green Candle
- Candle holder
- Inscribing Tool

- Money Oil *or regular olive oil if you cannot make this oil*
- Matches

Timing: Waxing Moon

Gather your required ingredients and prepare yourself for magick as you normally do. Holding your inscribing tool scratch into the candle how much money you need. Take the oil and anoint the candle, see yourself holding the money or depositing the check, see yourself paying your bills or getting the item, you need. When you are ready light the candle.

Money went now money comes

to me

opening me and my finances to

possibility

I can afford what I need and

desire

all this happens with this little

fire

green increases this little charm

*ensuring that there is no
financial harm*

bring me the money that I need

*money I can count on
guaranteed*

Let the candle burn out, if you can bury the remains in a potted plant or outside close to your front door.

A Money Potion

This drinkable money potion will help you bring extra money into your life. Though not entirely a spell there are words of power that can be chanted or intoned while brewing and drinking this potion to help money manifest in your life.

Items Needed:

- Tea Kettle to boil water

- A muslin bag, teaspoon, or ball- herbs can go inside.

- Real sugar- this is needed though the amount you add is up to you.

- Milk/creamer- optional

- tea cup or mug

The Tea: Here you have several options I know not everyone can make their own tea due to lack of garden space or lack of funds. A quick search provided Bigelow Herbal Mint Tea this would be a good substitute for the tea below. Be sure to always use edible herbs when making drinkable potions, use caution and make sure that it is medically safe for you to consume ALL ingredients always, you may need to check with your medical practitioner to insure your safety.

Or you can make your own tea:

- Fresh or Dried Mint Leaves- this makes up the bulk of the tea

- A Dash of Cinnamon or a small part of a cinnamon stick – a small amount will do this speed up the potion & spell.

- Red Clover Flowers – one or two will do you

- A small pinch of nutmeg- a very small amount

- A little bit of basil.

Timing: Whenever needed, this of course works better during the waxing moon phase.

As you place your water into the tea kettle think about your need for money: why do you need the money, how much do you need, by when do you need it. GET CLEAR ON YOUR GOALS!

As the water begins to warm up you can chant the main chant of this spell. Taking your herbs or tea bag hold the herbs in your hand and chant the main chant, when you are done place the herbs inside a bag, spoon, or, ball and place inside your tea cup or mug. When the water has reached a boil remove from heat and immediately pour over the herbs while saying the main chant of this spell. As the herbs seep in the water repeat the chant and build up power. Remove the herbs and add a touch of sugar, the sugar acts as a drawing agent bringing what you desire to you. You can add creamer or milk to suit your tastes. I suggest keeping the chant in mind the entire time you are enjoying your beverage. You can repeat this potion as often as you like.

THE MAIN CHANT:

As the water boils power grows strong

bringing abundance and money along

herbs of power steeped and brewed

it's magickal power the water imbued

bringing the money, I desire

by ___ I require (add in the time frame)

I drink the potion the magick's in me

as I will it so mote it be.

Money, Money, Money!

We could all use a bit more money right now. Especially with the holiday's looming. Let's work some money mojo together!

Items Needed:

- Green Candle
- Inscribing tool
- Matches
- Fire safe dish, cauldron, sink, tub etc.
- Aventurine
- Mint
- Olive Oil
- A small mixing jar/cup.

Timing: Waxing Moon.

Prepare yourself as you normally do for magick and set up your working space. Fill the small jar with oil and add in some mint, stir this potion clockwise with your dominate magickal hand. As you stir you can say these or similar words of intent:

Herb and oil mix as one

the magick has now begun

herb of green money you control

oil of abundance to make it whole

money and abundance come to me

as I will it so mote it be.

Take the candle now and inscribe the amount of money you need; this should be a reasonable number.

So, for example if you need enough money for your car payment and groceries don't ask for 1,000.00! (unless of course you drive a REALLY fancy car and are feeding an army!). The universe gives you want you need- not always what you want. Then taking the oil dip your dominant hands fingertips into the oil and anoint the candle with the oil.

Place the candle in a fire safe dish/cauldron or sink, there is potential for this candle to burn higher and wider than other candles with the herbs from the oil on its sides. Lighting the candle say these or similar words:

What I need is written out

the time has come to bring it about

Herbs and oil and candle glow

makes my money multiply and grow

what I need is coming to me

as I will it so mote it be.

Let this candle burn out completely. Sometimes spells will need to be repeated several times this may be one of those spells.

A Holiday Shopping Spell

I hope everyone had a great holiday? If you are in the USA you are probably getting hammered by black Friday/cyber Monday ads (in your e-mails, tv commercials, text messages, newspapers, computer screens, etc.) The truth is unless you have been REALLY good about your holiday shopping you may be like me! Needing to get things now and up until the last minute. This little charm can be used to help you find the perfect gifts at affordable prices, for everyone you need to buy for! There are a couple of things to keep in mind:

1. Go to stores that are in your budget! Seriously if you can't afford a store- no spell will help you get over that.

2. Try really hard to spend money you have and not place things on credit. I know in some cases this won't be possible but do your best to keep the amount low that goes on the credit cards.

3. Have a clear idea of what your budget is! You don't need to break it down to each person to the penny but do know the MAX amount of money you are willing to spend on the holidays and have a rough idea of the allotment for each person. I will spend more on my son than my parents & friends. So, for me it's 50% to my son, 25% for my parents and 25% for my friends.

4. Keep in mind the traditional meaning of the holidays, it's not about gifts but about love & family. Come from a place of love and you can't go wrong.

Items Needed:

- A green pen or marker
- a piece of paper- a sheet of printer paper will do.
- crushed or powdered cinnamon
- a tea-light candle or a chime candle
- matches or a lighter
- A square of cloth
- A green ribbon or string (embroidery floss is okay here.)

Timing: Whenever shopping needs to get done!

Gather your required ingredients and set up a space that is pleasant but practical for you, there is no need to go all out on this little charm unless you choose too. You may also wish to prepare yourself as well, this is a good way to start off on a clean slate.

On the piece of paper at the top in bold letters write out the amount of money you have to spend on gifts. This is in green bold letters. Underneath in the center (be sure to leave room to write around the edges of the paper) write out the people you have to buy for, preferably in order of importance. As I mentioned above my son is my biggest expense so he would go at the top.

When you have crafted your list, around the outside of the paper write this charm:

Tyche Goddess of chance, help me with the shopping dance, bargains and sales are all I'll find, specialty gifts and one of a kind. The perfect gift for all I need, I know that you will help me succeed. My budget is set in stone and clear, just what I need you draw near.

Light your green candle and say out-loud the chant above. Drip some wax on the four corners of the paper, then quickly sprinkle some cinnamon on top. Take the paper and begin to fold it towards you, symbolically bringing it towards you, fold it 3, 6, or 9 times, whichever will make it small enough to find on the square of cloth. Place the folded paper on the square of cloth and sprinkle some more cinnamon on top. Take up the edges of the cloth and form a bundle. Tie up the edges with the green ribbon or floss. Place it in front of the burning candle let this sit there until the candle has burn out completely. Then place the charm bag inside your purse or pocket as you go out and begin holiday shopping.

Increase My Cash Spell

We need money and what are we to do? This spell:

Items Needed:

- Green items- construction paper, green glitter, Saint Patrick's Day decorations, etc.

- green or gold candle

- matches

- One citrine crystal

- highest denomination bill you can get broken into 10's or 5's & a dollar bill.

- olive oil- in a small bottle

- dried basil herb *easily obtainable at the supermarket, in the herb/baking section*

Timing: This spell will be most potent during the waxing moon at noon but do this whenever your need is sincere.

Gather the required items needed for this spell and decorate it to be green- you can include the decorations on your altar or working space. Prepare yourself as you normally would do for any magickal act, this could include taking a bath, or smudging yourself. Set out the money in a fan, placing the dollar bill at the end, & light your candle. Mix up the Olive oil & the basil using these or similar words:

Herb and oil mixed as one

blended and charged by the sun

Money comes with green and gold

cash and money will unfold.

As you mix your potion chant that little phrase, it will help focus your mind on the working at hand and build the power to send your spell out into the universe. After you have mixed your potion together, anoint your hands with the oil and begin to touch the bills, hold each one separately and think about the money coming to you and depositing it into your bank account. You could quietly focus on this or use the chant above as you anoint the money.

Let the money sit anointed with the candle burning, place the citrine crystal on the money fan and day dream about money coming to you. See the end result of the money you need. See yourself going to the ATM or bank teller requesting a bank statement see the bank account reading the amount you wish.

This is not a spell to make you rich, this is a spell to help if you have upcoming bills, expenses or if like me you wish to be able to purchase something special for someone's birthday yet not deplete your savings account. This is important to note this spell will not help you if you are not willing to do the work- work overtime, advertise your skills, listen to friends who may be in need who could give you a few bucks for helping them, every dime helps get you closer to your goals. Pick those pennies up…

Now the rest of this spell involves some patience, each week I want you to deposit one of those higher-ranking bills anointed with the magickal oil, deposit it into your saving account/checking account. The dollar I want you to give that to a charity of some kind, a collection box, or a homeless individual in need of some money themselves, hand it over with love. You will see an improvement of your money- if needed repeat this spell. The citrine crystal is a talisman use it, carry it with you, take it to jobs, or out in public- be open to the universe.

A Spell for Employment

Items needed:

- Two small pieces of green fabric (or one medium sized piece)
- needle
- thread
- green ribbon or embroidery floss
- an aventurine stone
- Fool's gold/ Pyrite
- moss agate
- two bay leaves
- a pen (a small tip permanent marker better)
- a piece of a cinnamon stick
- Oregano
- Thyme
- Paprika
- some powdered sugar
- Piece of paper
- green candle
- matches

- fireproof dish

Gather required items.

Take the piece of fabric and lay it out, if you have decided to use two pieces and make a small bag then gather needle and thread. Make a small bag if that is what you have decided to do. If you have decided to make a scoop up pouch with a medium piece of fabric then just lay that out. Once you have crafted the bag; in a bowl mix together, your herbal ingredients.

Make a circle out of the powdered sugar making sure you leave enough room to add in your candle, the fire proof container and the finished charm bag once you are finished. Light your candle & connect with it for a moment it is lighting the way towards the manifestation of your job.

Take one bay leaf and crush it up the best you can into the bowl while thinking of the job you are looking to get. Bay leaves not only bring wealth but they are the wish granters of the plant world. That is why we are keeping one aside for the written wish.

Next add in the cinnamon stick, the oregano, the paprika, and thyme. Now i like to use thyme when I want to speed things up a bit.

Once you have this mixture of mixed herbs and spices in your bowl, Light your green candle. sit there for a moment and focus on your goal, start to really mix your herbs together while feeling their energies assisting you in your goal of getting a job. Talk to them as if they are your friends because they are. They are one of your unseen helpers here.

Once you have empowered your herbal mixture pick up the crystals and hold them in your hand. Crystals are also helpers; their vibration will help us attain our goal. connect with them as best you can and ask them to help draw to you the perfect job.

Add the herbal mixture and crystals and place them either inside the bag you have sewn or on top of the medium sized piece of fabric leaving room for the outer edges to be brought up to form a small bag.

Take the pen/marker and write your goal on the bay leaf and slip of paper.

"I want _____"

hold the bay leaf in your hand and really connect with it and ask it to help you bring your goal to fruition. once you have empowered your bay leaf, burn the leaf in the green candle, while smudging the piece of paper with the smoke of the burning bay leaf.

Add this slip of paper into the herbal mixture and crystals on top of the piece of green fabric. gather up the edges of the fabric, and tie the bag closed nine knots. stating your goal with each knot. Hold the completed bag in your hand and pass it over the candle (or pass the candle over the bag) several times empower it with the candles fire.

Hold this charm bag in your hand, this is your unseen helper that will allow you to manifest your goals, as you send out your resume, rub this bag over your resumes empowering them, tuck this bag in your pocket or purse during interviews.

If your feeling doubt about your ability to manifest your goals, light a green candle and connect with this charm bag again.

Money Oil

This formula can be combined with candle magick, mojo magick, employment needs etc.…

Items Needed:

- Tonka beans
- Dried mint

- patchouli oil
- amber oil
- a jar with a lid
- Aventurine crystal chip- this needs to fit into the bottle.
- pyrite
- powdered myrrh resin
- Mortar and Pestle
- green candle
- matches
- an incense of your choice- optional
- a carrier oil (olive oil, jojoba oil, sunflower oil- be sure to consult a reference to the shelf life of these oils)

Gather your ingredients and place your candle in a holder, it is up to you if you want to work in a circle or not.

Put your jar with a tight-fitting lid in the center of your working space with your candle nearby. Light your candle with a statement of intent, such as this:

Candle burning strong and steady, to make a magickal formula good and ready, money and prosperity comes to me, just as easily as can be.

You can chant this or a similar chant as you create this potion.

Put your mint, Tonka beans, myrrh resin, into the mortar and pestle and grind to a fine powder. When you are finished run your fingers, wand, or athame through this mixture empowering it with secret words of power, you can draw a symbol and maybe add a drop (just a drop) of wax on the mixture. Funnel these items into your bottle.

Hold your aventurine crystal in your hands empowering it just as you did with the herbal mixture. Place it within your jar.

Then cover the herbal mixture and stone with the carrier oil.

Add in several drops of Patchouli oil, amber oil and any special oils you may have linked to money.

Hold the bottle in your hands and breath it to life, while chanting or speaking your chosen phrase of power blow your final words into the bottle to empower it further.

Place next to the candle, and let the candle burn out. Place any candle remains inside the bottle.

A Fortune Chant

This fun little fortune chant can be used for any type of fortune work!

Fortuna, Fortuna bring to me

Wealth and overflowing money

Conclusion

I hope you have learned a lot with this magickal collection of spells, recipes, and chants. This book has been a real pleasure to make; a collection of spells and witchery over 5 years in the making! I am honored that you choose to get this book. I'd love to hear what you think! Shoot me an email questions@katiemcbrien.com and let me know what you think!

About Katie

Katie McBrien is a practicing Witch & Shamanic Practitioner located in Pennsylvania. Katie is a Sea Priestess and Sea Shaman, going back and forth between Pennsylvania and New Jersey and is available for spiritual coaching with an emphasis on helping witches find their own brand of magick and has a shamanic healing practice.

Katie spends her time working on her website, writing blogs, hanging out in her Facebook group.

Katie runs her popular nautically themed website www.seapriestess.org and her Facebook group: https://www.facebook.com/groups/theseapriestess

Printed in Dunstable, United Kingdom